Leaders Who Inspire

Stories of Foreign-Born University Presidents

Krishna Bista

STAR Scholars

Published by

STAR Scholars

PO Box: 374, Baltimore, Maryland

First Reader Series

ISBN: 978-1-957480-23-7 LCCN: 2023938860

Library of Congress

US Programs, Law, and Literature Division |Cataloging in Publication Program

101 Independence Avenue, S.E. Washington, DC 20540-4283

Printed in the United States of America

Typsett: Guru Mantra

Cover Design: Sahar Aghasafari

This book is designed for classroom use and can be used for educational purposes without additional permission. Its stories and images were carefully selected with input from scholars. Some of the contents in this book were developed using AI technology, specifically ChatGPT, to assist in editing and making the content suitable for young readers. Published by STAR Scholars, a non-profit organization based in Baltimore, Maryland, this book is limited in print and intended to inspire young learners to make a positive impact in their communities and beyond.

starscholars.org

Praises for the book

"A thrilling look at brave leaders from around the world who've made a difference in education. *Leaders Who Inspire* is a wonderful reminder to young readers that our dreams have no borders." ***Dr. Uttam Gaulee,*** *Morgan State University, Maryland*

"A brilliant read! 'It enlightens children about the power of dreams. A must-have for our young ones' bookshelf!" ***Dr. Ling Gao LeBeau,*** *Syracuse University, New York*

Explore the "First Readers" series and help children embark on thrilling adventures while fostering a lifelong love for reading.

https://www.ojed.org/index.php/gsm/catalog/category/youngreaders

About the book

Leaders Who Inspire: Stories of Foreign-Born University Presidents is a captivating book that introduces young readers to the remarkable stories of foreign-born college and university presidents. Through engaging narratives, readers will discover the inspiring journeys of leaders like Shirley M. Tilghman, Ángel Cabrera, A. Gabriel Esteban, and Renu Khator, who have made a significant impact on education in the United States.The book highlights the importance of diversity and inclusivity in educational institutions, showing how these leaders have transformed their campuses into welcoming spaces for students from all backgrounds. Readers will learn about the challenges these leaders faced, their unwavering determination, and their passion for empowering students to succeed.

Leaders Who Inspire celebrates the power of education and the strength that comes from embracing diversity. It encourages readers to believe in themselves, pursue their dreams, and make a positive impact in their own lives and communities.

About the author

Krishna Bista teaches at Morgan State University in Maryland and writes about what it's like to be a college student and how students can have exciting experiences by studying in different countries. Dr. Bista has written many books and articles about college student experiences.

Contents

Chapter 1

Dr. Shirley M. Tilghman

A Journey from Toronto to Princeton's Presidency

Born in the bustling city of Toronto, Canada, Dr. Shirley M. Tilghman was not just any ordinary girl. With a passion for science and an unstoppable spirit, she grew up to be a pioneering molecular biologist and the first female president of Princeton University, one of the most prestigious universities in the United States.

Dr. Tilghman's educational journey took her from Queen's University in Canada to the University of Pennsylvania in the United States, where she delved into the fascinating world of molecular biology. She was always captivated by the complexities of genes and

DNA, the tiny building blocks that make us who we are.

Dr. Shirley M. Tilghman

Her scientific discoveries have been monumental. She was part of the team that first cloned mammalian genes, a breakthrough that has greatly influenced genetics and medical research. Her contributions to science have been recognized in several books, and her research papers are considered crucial in her field.

In 2001, Dr. Tilghman made history by becoming the first woman president of Princeton University. Under her presidency, she made the university a more inclusive place, promoting diversity and equality. She initiated significant changes, like increasing financial aid for students, showing her commitment to making education accessible to all.

Dr. Tilghman's story teaches us that with dedication and perseverance, we can overcome obstacles and achieve our dreams. Regardless of where we're born or what our passions are, we all have the potential to make a significant impact.

Reflective Questions:

1. How did Dr. Tilghman's education contribute to her achievements in molecular

biology? (Understanding)

2. What challenges did she face as a woman in science, and how did she overcome them? (Analyzing)

3. In what ways did Dr. Tilghman improve Princeton University during her presidency? (Evaluating)

4. How does Dr. Tilghman's story inspire you to follow your passion? (Applying)

5. If you could design a science experiment with Dr. Tilghman, what would it be? (Creating)

Chapter 2

Dr. Renu Khator

An Indian Immigrant's Journey to Lead the University of Houston

A young girl born in Farrukhabad, a small town in Uttar Pradesh, India, had a dream. That girl was Renu Khator, who would grow up to become a leading figure in American higher education. Despite being expected to marry at a young age, Renu had other plans. She was determined to continue her education. She obtained her Bachelor's degree from Kanpur University in India. Later, she moved to the United States with her husband, where she achieved a Master's degree and a Ph.D. in Political Science from Purdue University.

In 2008, Dr. Khator made history by becoming the first female chancellor in Texas and the first

Indian immigrant to lead a comprehensive research university in the U.S. As the president of the University of Houston and chancellor of the University of Houston System, she has transformed the institution into a top-tier, nationally recognized university.

Dr. Renu Khator

Under her leadership, the University of Houston achieved Tier One status for the highest research activity from the Carnegie Foundation, opened Houston's first medical school in over 40 years, and secured a chapter of the prestigious Phi Beta Kappa honor society. She also helped raise more than $1 billion for the "Here, We Go" campaign and expanded the university's athletic facilities and programs, including an invitation to join the Big 12 Conference.

Dr. Khator has received numerous awards and recognitions throughout her career, including being inducted into the Texas Women's Hall of Fame, receiving the Pravasi Bharatiya Samman from the President of India, and being elected to the American Academy of Arts and Sciences.

Her incredible journey reminds us all that with dedication, hard work, and a commitment to excellence, we can overcome barriers and achieve our dreams.

Questions for Reflection:

1. What were some of Dr. Khator's most significant accomplishments at the University of Houston?

2. How did Dr. Khator's background and experiences contribute to her success in higher education?

3. What are some ways Dr. Khator has improved the University of Houston and its reputation?

4. Why is it important to recognize Dr. Khator's achievements as the first female chancellor in Texas and the first Indian immigrant to lead a comprehensive research university in the U.S.?

5. If you could ask Dr. Khator for advice on achieving success, what would you want to know?

Chapter 3

Dr. Farnam Jahanian

An Inspiring Journey from Iran to Carnegie Mellon University's Presidency

Farnam Jahanian's life story is a profound example of the power of resilience, hard work, and the pursuit of knowledge. Born in Tehran, Iran, he relocated to the United States as a teenager. Graduating from high school in San Antonio, Texas, he navigated the challenges of a new culture, language, and education system.

Farnam pursued his passion for computer science at the University of Texas, achieving a Bachelor's degree, a Master's degree, and a PhD. His career is a compelling narrative of academic excellence, entrepreneurial spirit, and transformative leadership. He demonstrated his intellectual prowess as a professor at the University of Michigan, his innovative thinking as co-founder of the tech company Arbor Networks, and his strategic leadership as director of the National Science Foundation's Computer and Information Science and Engineering Directorate.

Dr. Farnam Jahanian

In 2014, Farnam joined Carnegie Mellon University (CMU), initially serving as vice president for research, before being appointed the 10th president in 2018. During his tenure, he has elevated CMU's status as a global leader in research and education, launching innovative research centers, pioneering the world's first undergraduate major in artificial intelligence, and fostering cross-disciplinary collaborations. He has also spearheaded the largest expansion of CMU's campus infrastructure in its history and emphasized the importance of diversity, equity, and inclusion.

Farnam's profound contributions to computer science, especially in distributed computing and network security, have earned him numerous accolades. He is a fellow of esteemed organizations such as the Association for Computing Machinery, the Institute of Electrical and Electronics Engineers, and the American Association for the Advancement of Science.

Dr. Farnam Jahanian's journey—from a young Iranian immigrant to a celebrated scholar, tech entrepreneur, and transformative higher education leader—is a testament to the transformative power of education and tenacity. His life echoes the sentiment that with unwavering determination and a pursuit of knowledge, one can transcend barriers and reach unprecedented heights.

Questions for Reflection:

1. Can you list some of Dr. Jahanian's major accomplishments and positions in his career? (Remembering)

2. How would you describe the influence of Dr. Jahanian's contributions on Internet stability and security? (Understanding)

3. Based on Dr. Jahanian's journey, how would you set your own educational and career goals? (Applying)

4. What factors in Dr. Jahanian's life contributed to his success in academia and entrepreneurship? (Analyzing)

5. How would you assess Dr. Jahanian's approach to balancing his academic pursuits and entrepreneurial initiatives? (Evaluating)

6. Inspired by Dr. Jahanian's work, what innovative ideas could you propose to advance the fields of computer science and education? (Creating)

Chapter 4

Dr. Ángel Cabrera

A Journey from Madrid to Georgia Tech Presidency

Born on August 5, 1967, in Madrid, Ángel Cabrera Izquierdo, a man of unyielding determination and boundless curiosity, would grow up to make history as the first Spanish-born president of an American university. His journey to leadership began with a passion for learning, earning a telecommunications engineering degree from Universidad Politécnica de Madrid, followed by an MS and a Ph.D. in cognitive psychology from Georgia Institute of Technology as a Fulbright Scholar.

Dr. Cabrera's thirst for knowledge and dedication to education led him to become a renowned scholar, with influential work in learning, management, and leadership. As a scholar, he co-authored a seminal paper on knowledge-sharing, a testament to his belief in the power of shared expertise and ideas. His academic journey led him to various leadership roles, including the deanship of IE Business School, presidency of Thunderbird School of Global Management, and George Mason University before becoming the 12th President of Georgia Institute of Technology.

Dr. Cabrera's transformative leadership at George Mason University resulted in numerous advancements, including a significant increase in student enrollment, the establishment of multiple research centers, and winning a national competition to establish a Department of Homeland Security Center of Excellence. His accomplishments earned him worldwide recognition, with honors including the World Economic Forum's Global Leader for

Tomorrow in 2002 and a Great Immigrant by Carnegie Corporation in 2017.

Dr. Ángel Cabrera

Today, as the president of Georgia Institute of Technology, Dr. Cabrera continues to inspire. He bravely led the Institute through the challenges of the Covid-19 pandemic, breaking records in student applications, enrollment, graduation rates, and research awards. His story teaches us the power of perseverance, the importance of education, and the impact one person can make when they dedicate their life to serving others.

Questions for Reflection:

1. How did Ángel Cabrera's educational background contribute to his leadership roles in various universities? (Analyzing)

2. What qualities do you think make Ángel Cabrera an effective leader? (Evaluating)

3. How has Ángel Cabrera made a significant impact on the institutions he has led? (Understanding)

4. Imagine you are Ángel Cabrera. How would you handle the challenges brought by the Covid-19 pandemic? (Applying)

5. What lessons can you learn from Ángel Cabrera's journey and apply to your own life goals? (Creating)

Chapter 5

Dr. Satish K. Tripathi

From Rural India to the Presidency of the University at Buffalo

Satish K. Tripathi's story is a true testament to the power of determination, hard work, and a thirst for knowledge. Born and raised in the small village of Patna in northeastern India, Tripathi's humble beginnings were a far cry from the prestigious academic positions he would later hold in the United States. His journey is a lesson for all children that no matter where you come from, you can reach the stars with dedication and a passion for learning.

Dr. Tripathi graduated at the top of his class from Banaras Hindu University (BHU) in India. His thirst for knowledge then led him to Canada, where he earned a doctorate in computer science and two master's degrees from the University of Toronto and the University of Alberta. His work ethic and love for computer science and statistics propelled him into a distinguished academic career.

Dr. Satish K. Tripathi

In 2011, Dr. Tripathi made history by becoming the first foreign-born president of the University at Buffalo (UB), the flagship of the State University of New York (SUNY) system. He led the university to achieve significant growth in research, student diversity, and an expanded international presence.

Tripathi's leadership extended beyond the confines of the university, serving on the boards of various prestigious organizations, highlighting his commitment to enhancing higher education and research. His efforts were recognized with honorary doctorates from the Indian Institute of Information Technology, Allahabad, and Brock University in Canada.

Dr. Tripathi's story is an inspiration for every child that dreams big. His journey teaches us that with hard work, dedication, and an insatiable curiosity, one can conquer even the most daunting challenges and reach the heights of success.

Questions for Reflection:

1. What were some of the early educational achievements of Satish K. Tripathi? (Remembering)

2. How did Tripathi contribute to the growth and development of the University at

Buffalo? (Understanding)

3. How would you apply Tripathi's approach to learning and education in your own life? (Applying)

4. Can you compare the education system in India, where Tripathi began his journey, with that of the United States, where he became a university president? (Analyzing)

5. What makes Tripathi's journey from a small village in India to becoming the president of a major American university inspiring? (Evaluating)

6. If you could ask Tripathi a question about his journey, what would it be? (Creating)

Chapter 6
Dr. Reginald DesRoches

A Journey from Haiti to Rice University's Presidency

Reginald DesRoches is a true pioneer, shattering stereotypes and blazing a trail of success in the field of engineering and academia. Born in Port-au-Prince, Haiti, DesRoches faced numerous obstacles on his path to becoming the first Black and foreign-born president of Rice University. His remarkable journey is a testament to the power of resilience, passion, and unwavering determination.

DesRoches' educational journey began in New York City, where he attended St. Francis Preparatory High School. His thirst for knowledge and love for engineering led him to the prestigious University of California, Berkeley, where he earned three degrees—a Bachelor of Science, a Master of Science, and a Doctorate in structural engineering.

Dr. Reginald DesRoches

Throughout his career, Dr. DesRoches has demonstrated a commitment to excellence and a passion for making a positive impact. As a civil engineer, his research and design of resilient infrastructure systems have earned him prestigious accolades, including induction into the National Academy of Engineering. DesRoches' work has focused on mitigating damage from natural disasters and other extreme conditions, showcasing his dedication to creating a safer and more resilient world.

In addition to his groundbreaking engineering contributions, Dr. DesRoches has proven himself as an exceptional academic leader. Prior to his presidency at Rice University, he served as provost and dean of engineering, spearheading innovative initiatives and providing leadership to renowned institutions of higher learning. His research interests and publications have garnered international recognition, and he has shared his expertise through presentations and collaborations worldwide.

DesRoches' story serves as an inspiration to all children, emphasizing the importance of education, resilience, and breaking down barriers. Through his accomplishments, he has shown that with hard work and determination, one can rise above adversity and achieve greatness.

Questions for Reflection :

1. What are some of the significant achievements of Reginald DesRoches in the field of engineering? (Remembering)

2. How did DesRoches break barriers and make history as the first Black and foreign-born president of Rice University? (Understanding)

3. Why is DesRoches' commitment to resilient infrastructure systems important for society? (Applying)

4. How did DesRoches demonstrate leadership and innovation during his tenure as provost and dean of engineering? (Analyzing)

5. What lessons can you learn from DesRoches' journey about perseverance and overcoming

obstacles? (Evaluating)

6. If you had the opportunity to meet Reginald DesRoches, what would you ask him about his experiences and accomplishments? (Creating)

Chapter 7

Dr. Subra Suresh

From India to Carnegie Mellon University's Presidency

In a world where possibilities are endless, one person's determination and passion can shape the future. Born in Chennai, India, Suresh's thirst for knowledge and passion for science guided him on a path of extraordinary achievements.

Suresh's educational journey took him from the Indian Institute of Technology (IIT) Madras, where he earned his Bachelor's degree in Engineering, to the Massachusetts Institute of Technology (MIT), where he obtained his Master's and Ph.D. degrees in Engineering. His relentless pursuit of knowledge led him to become a world-leading scholar in materials science and engineering, specializing in the mechanical behavior of materials at the atomic scale.

Dr. Subra Suresh

Throughout his illustrious career, Dr. Suresh has published groundbreaking research papers, authored influential books, and received numerous accolades for his contributions to the field of science. His work has significantly advanced our understanding of the mechanical properties of materials, laying the foundation for groundbreaking advancements in fields such as nanotechnology and bioengineering.

In recognition of his outstanding contributions, Dr. Suresh has received several honorary degrees from prestigious universities around the world. His dedication to scientific research and academic leadership has earned him numerous awards and honors. As the president of Carnegie Mellon University and later Nanyang Technological University (NTU) in Singapore, Dr. Suresh transformed these institutions into vibrant centers of innovation and excellence. He championed diversity, sustainability, and the integration of arts and sciences, fostering a nurturing environment for students and researchers. His efforts to bridge cultural, ethnic, and gender gaps have laid the foundation for a more inclusive and equitable scientific community.

Questions for Reflection :

1. What are some of the notable

educational achievements of Subra Suresh? (Remembering)

2. How has Suresh's research in materials science and engineering contributed to scientific advancements? (Understanding)

3. What are some of the honors and awards that Suresh has received for his contributions to the field of science? (Applying)

4. How did Suresh's leadership as the President of Carnegie Mellon University impact the institution? (Analyzing)

5. How has Suresh's work in interdisciplinary collaborations and promoting diversity influenced the academic community? (Evaluating)

6. If you could meet Subra Suresh, what would you ask him about his journey and achievements? (Creating)

Chapter 8

Dr. Pradeep Khosla

From India to the University of California, San Diego as a Chancellor

In a world brimming with possibilities, where dreams can shape the future, one person's determination can inspire generations to come. Meet Chancellor Pradeep Khosla, a visionary leader, educator, and champion of innovation. From his roots in India to his trailblazing role as the Chancellor of the University of California, San Diego (UCSD), Khosla's journey is a testament to the power of perseverance and the boundless potential within us all.

After completing his Bachelor's degree in Electrical Engineering from Indian Institute of Technology (IIT) in Kharagpur, Khosla pursued his Master's and Ph.D. degrees in Electrical and Computer Engineering at Carnegie Mellon University in the United States.

Pradeep Khosla

Dr. Khosla's passion for education and innovation led him to become a distinguished scholar, renowned for his research in robotics, computer-aided design, and wireless sensor networks. He has published numerous scientific articles and co-authored influential books in these fields, inspiring countless students and researchers worldwide.

Throughout his career, Dr. Khosla has received widespread recognition for his exceptional leadership and contributions to the field of engineering. He has been bestowed with honorary degrees from esteemed institutions and has received prestigious awards. As the Chancellor of UCSD, Dr. Khosla has transformed the university into a hub of innovation, diversity, and academic excellence. Under his visionary guidance, UCSD has embraced cutting-edge technologies and interdisciplinary collaboration, fostering an environment where students and researchers can explore, discover, and create. Khosla's commitment to sustainable practices has led to the implementation of groundbreaking initiatives in renewable energy and resource conservation, making UCSD a global leader in sustainability.

Beyond his role as a university leader, Chancellor Khosla is a strong advocate for access to education for all, irrespective of background or circumstance. He believes in the power of education to unlock the potential within each individual and create a more equitable society. His unwavering dedication to fostering diversity and inclusion has made UCSD a beacon of opportunity and innovation for students from diverse backgrounds.

Questions for Reflection:

1. What are some of the notable achievements and contributions of Chancellor Pradeep Khosla in the field of engineering? (Remembering)

2. How has Chancellor Khosla transformed UCSD into a hub of innovation and academic excellence? (Understanding)

3. What initiatives has Chancellor Khosla implemented to make UCSD a global leader in sustainability? (Applying)

4. Why does Chancellor Khosla believe in the power of education to create a more equitable

society? (Analyzing)

5. How can you be inspired by Chancellor Khosla's journey and contribute to creating a better future through education and innovation? (Creating)

Chapter 9

Dr. Gabriel Esteban

From the Philippines to Becoming the First Lay Leader of DePaul University

Every person's journey begins somewhere. For Dr. Gabriel Esteban, that beginning was in the sunny archipelago of the Philippines. Born and raised there, his love for education started at a young age. He studied mathematics and earned an MBA in the Philippines. Later, he received a prestigious Fujitsu Scholarship that took him to Chaminade University in Hawaii, where he learned about Japanese business studies. He pursued his dreams tirelessly, earning a Ph.D. in Business Administration from the University of California, Irvine. His path to education was not a straight line, but a winding road full of lessons and victories.

Dr. Gabriel Esteban

Dr. Esteban served as the President of Seton Hall University, demonstrating his leadership skills and dedication to higher education. His hard work and commitment didn't go unnoticed; he was honored as the next President of DePaul University, becoming the 12th person to hold this prestigious role. As a scholar, Dr. Esteban's academic contributions have been significant, penning numerous books that have enriched the field of business administration and inspired countless students.

But Dr. Esteban's journey wasn't just about reaching the top. It was about striving for excellence, pursuing knowledge, and making a difference. His story teaches us that no matter where we come from, we have the power to shape our own future and make a positive impact in the world. We just need to believe in ourselves, work hard, and never give up.

Dr. Esteban's life is a testament to the fact that the pursuit of knowledge is a lifelong journey, not a destination. So, wherever you are in your journey, remember to keep learning, keep dreaming, and most importantly, keep going!

Questions for Reflection:

1. How did Dr. Esteban's early life in

the Philippines influence his educational journey? (Understanding)

2. What are some of Dr. Esteban's significant achievements as a scholar and a university president? (Remembering)

3. Why do you think Dr. Esteban's journey can be considered inspirational? (Analyzing)

4. How might Dr. Esteban's story inspire you to pursue your own dreams? (Applying)

5. If you could speak with Dr. Esteban, what would you ask him about his journey? (Creating)

Chapter 10

Dr. Sabah Randhawa

A Journey from Pakistan to Western Washington University's Presidency

In Pakistan, a young boy Sabah dreamt of making a difference through education. Little did he know that his passion for learning would lead him on an incredible journey as an educator and an academic leader, eventually becoming the 14th President of Western Washington University.

Sabah's educational adventure began in Pakistan, where he earned a bachelor's degree in chemical engineering. His thirst for knowledge took him to the United States, where he pursued a master's degree in industrial engineering from Oregon State University (OSU). Driven by his dedication to learning, he obtained his doctorate in industrial engineering from Arizona State University.

Dr. Sabah Randhawa

Throughout his career, Dr. Randhawa has made significant contributions to the field of higher education. He served as the Provost and Executive Vice President at OSU, where he led the university through a period of remarkable growth. Under his guidance, OSU experienced surging student enrollment, expanded campus and educational programs, and the successful completion of a comprehensive fundraising campaign.

As the president of Western Washington University, Dr. Randhawa's top priority is advancing student success and inclusive excellence. He believes that education has the power to transform lives and strives to make it accessible, affordable, and attainable for all. He is particularly passionate about supporting underrepresented students, ensuring they have the resources and opportunities to thrive. Dr. Randhawa's remarkable journey teaches us the importance of education, leadership, and inclusivity. He inspires us to dream big and work hard to achieve our goals. Dream, learn, and make a difference!

Questions for reflections

1. What are some important leadership positions Dr. Randhawa held before becoming the President of Western Washington University?

2. How did Dr. Randhawa's educational background contribute to his success as an academic leader?

3. What are some of the achievements and growth experienced by Oregon State University under Dr. Randhawa's leadership?

4. Why is advancing student success and inclusive excellence a top priority for Dr. Randhawa at Western Washington University?

5. How does Dr. Randhawa's personal experience as a first-generation college student influence his commitment to making higher education more accessible?

Born Abroad, Leading in America

Inspiring Tales of Foreign-Born University Presidents

Did you know that some of the most esteemed leaders in colleges and universities across the United States were born in different countries? These incredible individuals have not only made a significant impact on education but have also shown us the power of diversity and embracing different cultures. Let's explore the inspiring journeys of a few foreign-born college and university presidents.

- Shirley M. Tilghman, born in Toronto, Canada, served as the President of Princeton University. She believed in the transformative power of education and worked tirelessly to make Princeton a welcoming place for students from all backgrounds. She once said, "Education is the key to unlocking the world, a passport to freedom."

- Ángel Cabrera, born in Madrid, Spain, became the President of both the Thunderbird School of Global Management and George Mason University. He dedicated his life to fostering global connections and encouraging students to become global citizens. Cabrera believes, "Education is the most powerful weapon you can use to change the world."

- Renu Khator, born in Farrukhabad, India, serves as the President of the University of Houston and the Chancellor of the University of Houston System. She is a trailblazer, breaking barriers and inspiring others to pursue their dreams. Khator once said, "Dream big, work hard, and stay focused. The sky is the limit!"

These exceptional leaders and many others have shown us that no matter where we come from, we can achieve great things through education and perseverance. They have made a lasting impact on the lives of countless students and have helped shape a brighter future for all.

Here is a list of some remarkable foreign-born college and university presidents:

A. Gabriel Esteban - President of DePaul University (Born in the Philippines)
Ángel Cabrera - President of George Mason University and the Georgia Institute of Technology (Born in Spain)
Satish K. Tripathi - President of the University at Buffalo, SUNY (Born in India)
David W. Pershing - President of the University of Utah (Born in Canada)
Michael Rao - President of Virginia Commonwealth University (Born in India)
Santa J. Ono - President of the University of

Cincinnati and the University of British Columbia (Born in Canada)

Morton Schapiro - President of Northwestern University (Born in Canada)

Lee C. Bollinger - President of Columbia University (Born in the United Kingdom)

These leaders have shown us that diversity enriches our educational institutions and brings forth innovative ideas. They inspire us to celebrate our differences and work together toward a brighter future.

Remember, young readers, your dreams know no boundaries. With hard work, determination, and a thirst for knowledge, you can achieve anything you set your mind to. Let these inspiring leaders guide you on your journey of discovery and success.

With education, determination, and an open mind, you too can make a difference in the world.

Can you think of

someone who inspires you and why do they inspire you?

Inspiring Story

Which story in the book did you find most inspiring and why?